The Thirteen Steps

To Realizing the Self as One with Pure Source Awareness

by Bruce Taylor

With Gratitude

This book would not exist without the support and guidance of everyone with whom I have shared time during this journey through life. There are too many to name here. Please know that I am deeply grateful to all of you.

I would particularly like to thank Joe Lavery for inspiring the creation of these steps, His Holiness Lungtok Tenpai Nyima for guiding me in relearning the nature of mind, John Milton for guiding me in gaining experiential knowledge of the human experience, and Javier Regueiro for his friendship and support in diving deep into my shadow side.

I would also like to thank the participants at the workshops in San Pedro, Guatemala where I first presented these steps. Your insights, feedback, and presence played a major role in shaping the contents of this book in a way that will hopefully make it more accessible to the reader.

Lastly, I would like to thank my wife, Carie, for her patience, Love, and support throughout the journey of creating both this book and 'The Way Home'.

I Love you all. Thank you.

Table of Contents

Before time, there was One. You are that One.

Introduction

The 'Thirteen Steps' provide a way to realize the Self as One with pure Source awareness. The benefits of doing so are immeasurable. You will have direct experience of knowing who you are, will have returned 'home', will be free of the world of suffering, and will have a deep sense of inner peace, Love, harmony, and joy. You will be a shining light in a world of darkness and will be a blessing to everyone you meet.

However, achieving oneness with Source may feel daunting to you and you may not know if you want to connect all the way back to Source. You may be enjoying this world of form and feel drawn to remain as a player on the stage of life; at least for the time being. For this reason, we have divided the thirteen steps into three parts.

The first part is for everyone who wishes to achieve an inner state of peace, harmony, and Love. It can be completed by anyone regardless of their chosen faith, beliefs, and occupation. You can do these steps while living your daily life and you do not have to leave your loved ones behind. Once you begin, you won't have to wait long to start reaping the benefits. You will almost immediately begin to receive glimpses of inner peace and, over time, you will come to feel at peace regardless of what is happening in the world around you. After completing this part, you will:

- have discovered that you are a spiritual being having a human experience;
- have connected to your inner guide;
- have removed the barriers to Love from inside your being; and,
- be free to live your life from an inner state of peace, harmony, and divine Love.

You will then find that the people and events that you draw into your life will reflect your inner state. Your interactions with people will be more peaceful and Loving.

The second part of the 'Thirteen Steps' is for those who wish to fulfill their soul purpose. At first glance, it may seem like a no-brainer that you would want to do this but it is not quite that simple. Your soul purpose can only be revealed to you by your higher self (or soul) and can only be completed by your higher self. As long as you remain identified with your mind and body then you cannot fulfill your soul purpose. Thus, this part of the 'Thirteen Steps' will ask you to turn control of your life over to your higher self. Only then will you be able to complete your soul purpose and be free to act solely from divine Love. Surrendering to your higher self will require a wholehearted commitment to being willing to give up everything that you think you know in order to discover the essence of who you truly are.

The third part of the 'Thirteen Steps' is for those who feel drawn to have the oceanic experience of becoming one with pure Source awareness. When you merge back into Source, it merges with you. You become one with everything, and you are the field of awareness that is infusing everything in this world of form. You are everywhere at once and yet, 'you' are no longer there. Awareness simply is. You will have found your way 'home'. You can have this experience before leaving the body. You will then be free of all illusions and all suffering. You will be a blessing to all.

We recommend that you read through all of the steps before beginning. This will give you an overview of the overall process and will help you to understand the interdependencies between the various steps.

The steps are more circular than sequential and you will find yourself moving through many steps simultaneously. It is not necessary to master one step before moving on to the subsequent ones. You will often find that you will gain mastery over a step by working through the remaining ones. For example, the steps of 'Cultivating a Daily Spiritual Practice', 'Developing Trust in your own Inner Guide', and 'Cultivating Mindful Awareness' are the foundation on which the rest of the program is built. You will strengthen your mastery over these steps through working through other steps such as 'Look in the Mirror and Find your way Home'. That latter step will take you ever deeper into yourself and, the deeper you go, the more meditative strength, trust, and awareness you are going to need. We recommend that you develop a basic proficiency with each step and then move on to the subsequent ones.

Warning: This journey will destroy all of the illusions that you hold about yourself and this world.

Before you begin, there is a warning that comes with embarking upon this journey. This thirteen step process is intended for those who are ready to delve inwards in order to discover the essence of who they truly are. This inner journey of freeing yourself from the false will invite you to both heal your shadow side and turn control of your life over to your higher self. Both can be challenging parts of your journey.

In Part one, you will be working towards achieving an inner state of peace, harmony, and Love. Reaching that state will involve removing the barriers inside yourself to being able to exist in that state always. Those barriers include your shadow side and surfacing your shadow can result in bouts of depression, frustration, and other emotions. Depression in particular may occur when your mind struggles to accept the contents of your shadow side and goes into resistance to it. It is challenging to heal your shadow side and the reward for doing so is an ever-deepening sense of inner peace. Is that reward enough for you to face yourself? Only you know.

In part two, you will be turning control of your life over to your higher self and that process often results in a form of spiritual madness. The madness arises due to an inner war between your mind and your higher self for control over your life. This inner battle is often referred to as the dark night of the soul. We describe a way to pass through the dark night in step 10. It can be challenging to face your own dark night but the reward for doing so is immeasurable; you.

Remember, you are not alone. The 'Thirteen Steps' are part of the broader 'The Way Home' program which has been created to provide you with support and guidance throughout your journey. It includes the 'Thirteen Steps', a book on self-healing, workshops, retreats, and communal living space. You do have to walk your own unique path but you do not have to walk it alone.

Okay, are you ready to begin? The 'Thirteen Steps' are listed on the next page. The subsequent chapters then describe each step.

The Thirteen Steps

To Realizing the Self as One with Pure Source Awareness

Part One: Cultivate an Inner State of Peace, Harmony, & Love

1. Open to the Possibility that you are a Spiritual Being having a Human experience.

2. Cultivate a daily Spiritual Practice.

3. Develop Trust in your own Inner Guide.

4. Cultivate Mindful Awareness.

5. Relax, life is a journey to be enjoyed not a struggle to be endured.

6. Cultivate Love, Forgiveness, Compassion, Acceptance, and Gratitude.

7. Commit to Achieving Inner Peace, Harmony, and Love.

8. Look in the Mirror and Remove the Barriers to Love.

Part Two: Fulfill your Soul Purpose

9. Commit to turning control of your Life over to your Higher Self.

10. Accept that spiritual madness is a normal part of the journey 'home' and that the madness can be passed through.

11. Surrender to your Higher Self.

12. Fulfill your Soul Purpose.

Part Three: Achieve Self-Realization

13. Realize the Self as One with Pure Source Awareness.

"Your task is not to seek for Love, but merely to seek and find all the barriers within yourself that you have built against it."
— Jalal ad Din Muhammad Rumi

Part One: Cultivate Peace, Harmony, and Love

1. Open to the Possibility that you are a Spiritual Being having a Human experience.

This step asks you to open yourself up to the possibility that you are more than just the body and mind, and that you are actually a spiritual being having a human experience.

What does that mean? It means that we all have an aspect of ourselves that exists beyond the physical body. That aspect of us has been referred to by many beautiful beings throughout time and has been given names such as witnessing consciousness, soul, higher self, and inner guide. We have chosen to refer to it with the interchangeable terms of soul, inner guide, and higher self. Regardless of the name you prefer, we ask you to be open to the possibility that such a 'spiritual' aspect of you does indeed exist.

We would like to briefly touch on the content of parts two and three of the 'Thirteen Steps' in order to give you an idea of how your higher self could exist. This is for your information only and please don't worry about having to completely understand it at this point on your journey.

There is a field of energy that permeates absolutely everything in our physical world (the world of form). All forms arise out of it and return to it. This field has been given many names: Tao, Source, Holy Spirit, Awareness, Divine Love, God, Universal Consciousness, and more. We have chosen to use the term 'pure Source awareness' (or Source for short) as our name for that field, and the term 'Divine Love' for the energy of that field. We are literally swimming in an ocean of divine Love and life is divine Love in action. Your higher self, or soul, was seeded from that field of pure Source awareness and it also carries the energy of divine Love.

Basically, we, as human beings, have a body, mind, and soul, and we exist within a field of pure Source awareness. That field is the source of who we all are and merging back into it enables us to experience being all that is. Many people are living under the illusion that they are solely the mind and body, and have lost touch with the essence of who they truly are. It does not have to remain that way. In part two, we will show you a process for surrendering to your higher self and, in part three, we will describe the oceanic experience of retuning all the way 'home' to Source. We call that latter experience 'Oneness' or 'Realizing the Self as One with Pure Source Awareness'.

However, all of that can wait for later. For now, we are focused on the first part of the 'Thirteen Steps', achieving an inner state of peace, harmony, and Love. The process for achieving that state begins with your accepting the possibility that you do indeed have a higher self and that the energy of your higher self is divine Love. It is the existence of this aspect of you that makes you a spiritual being having a human experience.

When you take this first step of accepting that possibility, you are opening the door to Love. The remaining steps in this first part of the 'Thirteen Steps' will show you how to walk through that door. They will guide you through the process of connecting to your higher self and removing everything from inside your being that is preventing you from experiencing divine Love.

Okay, please don't believe any of this. All we ask is that you remain open to it being possible and then to find out for yourself if it is true for you.

Are you open to the possibility that you are a spiritual being having a human experience?

2.   Cultivate a daily Spiritual Practice.

It is important to cultivate a daily spiritual practice in order to discover that there is more to you than just the body and mind. The intent of this daily practice is to allow your mind to fall silent so that you can feel yourself as the witnessing consciousness that inhabits the body. This will give you the immediate benefit of feeling the inner peace that comes from a silent mind. It will also give you the longer-term benefit of experiencing that you are an energetic being having a human experience. You will be on your way 'home'.

We recommend that you set aside a minimum of twenty minutes per day for your spiritual practice. It could include meditation, walks in nature, yoga, surfing, chopping vegetables, or any other activity that supports you in allowing your mind to fall silent. It does not include activities that feed your rational mind such as reading books or scriptures, listening to any recordings of dialogues or music, or entering into conversations with other people. The rule of thumb is to exclude everything that either causes you to think or entertains your mind. You can do these other activities for the rest of the day if you like but do not include them in your spiritual practice.

It can be difficult at first to allow the mind to fall silent and you may find it beneficial to take courses that open you up to the possibility that you are an energetic being. If you are struggling with your spiritual practice then we recommend enrolling in programs such as Hatha yoga, dream work, spiritual tools, energy healing, and, meditation retreats.

3.   Develop Trust in your own Inner Guide.

Cultivating trust in your inner guide is the most important step of them all. You have a unique path to follow and only your inner guide knows your way. We know from our own personal experience that you will likely stumble around in the dark if you don't cultivate this trust.

The inner guide that we are referring to is the witnessing consciousness that you are learning to access through your daily spiritual practice. It goes by different names: the intuitive mind, the higher self, inner knowingness, inner guide, the 'witness', the soul, and many more. Learning to hear the guidance that it is giving you, and then following that guidance, is the core of this program. Cultivating trust in your inner guide will allow you to find your own unique path, and to face all of the obstacles to Love that are placed in your way as you walk your path.

Unfortunately, many people have forgotten that they have an inner guide. The following quote from Bob Samples (which is often attributed to Albert Einstein) highlights this issue:

"The intuitive mind is a sacred gift and the rational mind is a faithful servant. We have created a society that honors the servant and has forgotten the gift." (1)

It is time to remember the gift (intuitive mind or inner guide). We need it to find our way home. In western society, this part of us has often been forgotten but all is not lost. Our inner guides are patiently waiting for us to stop giving control of our lives over to the rational mind (honoring the servant) and to turn our awareness back to them for guidance. This step asks you to do that.

Your daily spiritual practice will support you in allowing your mind to fall silent so that you can connect to your inner guide. It takes patience and diligence to learn how to hear the messages that your inner guide is communicating to you. We recommend that you try one or more of the following techniques for connecting to your inner guide.

Automatic Writing – write down everything that is in your mind until your mind falls silent, and then keep writing. Eventually you will be writing words without knowing how sentences are going to end and without having any idea what you are writing about. At that point, you are doing 'automatic writing' and you will be receiving messages from your inner guide.

Insight meditation – ask yourself a question that you would like your inner guide to answer and then let it go. Sit in meditation, allow your mind to fall silent, and patiently wait. Your inner guide may choose to provide you with insights on the answer to your question.

Making choices - practice trusting your intuition over your rational mind when it comes to the choices you make in your life; including things such as which direction to walk through town, which book to read, which meal to order, and so on.

Dream Work – ask your dreams to guide you. Write down a question on a piece of paper and leave it on your bedside table. Repeat the question to yourself as you are falling asleep and ask your dreams to give you an answer. Write down any dreams that you have during the night and interpret them in the morning. You can use any method of interpreting your dreams because, as long as you use the same method consistently, your inner guide will adapt its messages to your chosen method.

Once you have begun listening to the messages from your inner guide, it will start to work more actively with you and will point you towards your own unique path 'home'. Don't be attached to the guidance that it gives you as having to come in any specific way. It will come through a variety of forms, messengers, and signals. The rule of thumb to use is that, if something comes into your life three times then it is time to pay attention.

Your challenge then is to act on the messages from your inner guide. Your rational mind may not like what your inner guide is asking you to do and it may use all kinds of logical arguments to stop you. You will need to learn to ignore logic and to follow your inner guide regardless of what your rational mind thinks. We recommend that you start with small choices, such as what book to read, rather than life changing ones.

4. Cultivate Mindful Awareness.

Cultivating Mindful awareness will liberate you from being a prisoner in your own mind. It will lay the foundation for your being able to remove the barriers inside you to Love.

Mindful awareness is one of the core practices of Buddhism. When you are mindful, you are remaining in the present moment. One way to understand mindfulness is to look at your ability to recall events. If you are able to remember an event clearly then you were mindful during that event. If you are not able to remember it clearly then you were distracted and were not mindful.

Awareness is being aware of everything going on both inside you and all around you in any given moment. It includes the five main senses (what you hear, see, smell, feel, and taste), your inner emotional state, your thoughts, and any other senses, such as clairsentience, that you have developed. For this process, the emphasis for your awareness practice is primarily on your inner world. You are bringing awareness to what is happening inside you in reaction to events that you are encountering in your daily life.

The combination of being mindful and having awareness is called Mindful Awareness. It is a meditative practice that allows you to remain present and aware of your inner state of being at all times and in all situations, while also remaining aware of everything around you.

Your journey 'home' is a journey inwards and it is your inner reaction to external events that matters on this journey, not the external events. If you can bring present time awareness to your inner reactions, without getting attached to the thoughts and emotions that arise from them, then you can choose to respond to life rather than react to it. You will be free from being a prisoner of your fears, conditioning, traumas, and ego-based desires. You haven't removed them from your being but you are free of reacting from them.

Mindful awareness is also a prerequisite to being able to 'Look in the Mirror and find your way Home' (step eight). It gives you separation from your thoughts and emotions, and allows you to watch the dramas of life unfold rather than getting caught up in them. You are able to observe the play rather than being an actor in it. You are able to look in the mirror. We digress, that can all wait until you get to step eight.

We recommend that you find someone to teach you mindful awareness in a formal course setting. It is a relatively simple concept to understand but can be challenging to put into practice. One option for developing an experiential understanding of mindful awareness would be to attend a ten day Vipassana meditation retreat.

We have found that learning mindful awareness is a gradual process. At first you may find that you can remain mindfully aware when weak emotions arise in you but that you still get lost in your stronger emotions. This is to be expected and we recommend that you do not be too hard on yourself. Please remember to cultivate compassion for you. We suggest that you move on to the subsequent steps after taking a course such as Vipassana meditation. You can then practice being mindfully aware in real life situations while also gaining the benefit of doing work on yourself. Over time, you will find that you are able to remain mindfully aware in the face of stronger and stronger emotions.

5.   Relax, life is a journey to be enjoyed not a struggle to be endured.

Remember not to take any of this too seriously. Relax, life is a journey to be enjoyed not a struggle to be endured.

Feeling relaxed is our natural state of being. It is only when we get lost in our fears, false beliefs, emotional traumas, and desires that we begin to tense up. These are the barriers to Love and, in the next few steps, we will be exploring how to find those barriers and then remove them. That process can be emotionally challenging at times and it is important to remember to relax as much as possible, regardless of what is going on inside you. The good news is that you will find yourself becoming more and more relaxed as you progress through these steps and connect back to your essential nature.

It may be difficult for you to feel relaxed when confronted with the events of daily life and that is where cultivating trust in your inner guide helps. As you learn to trust your inner guide, you will find yourself coming to accept that your inner guide is working hard to bring you all of the experiences that you need in order to find your way 'home'. You will also begin to understand that your inner guide only brings experiences into your life once you are ready to face them. As you begin to know all of this for yourself, you will find yourself better able to remain relaxed and at ease regardless of what is happening in and around you.

The combination of a spiritual practice, cultivating trust, learning mindful awareness, and doing your best to remain relaxed at all times will allow you to face any challenge that come your way.

One of the additional benefits of becoming deeply relaxed is that an inner joy may just poke its head out to find out what is going on.

6. **Cultivate Love, Compassion, Forgiveness, Acceptance, and Gratitude.**

This step contains the values that facilitate the healing process you will be embarking upon in step eight, Removing the Barriers to Love. We recommend that you embrace them throughout your journey.

- **Love** – Divine Love is the type of Love that you are moving towards.

    We define three separate and distinct types of love: ego-based love; heart-based love; and, divine Love. Ego-based love comes from the desire for self-gratification. It includes things such as I love chocolate because it tastes good, I love you because you make me happy, and I love a bubble bath because it feels good. Heart-based love is other centered. It is about wanting what's best for another. This is also a game of the ego as you are imposing your ego's beliefs of what is best onto another. These first two types of love are generated by the mind and do not have the purity of

Divine Love.

Divine Love is a state of being that arises when your mind falls silent. The only thing that blocks you from existing as Love is your becoming lost in your ego. The components of your ego (your fears, desires, beliefs, and emotional traumas) are known as your barriers to Love because your becoming identified with any one of them prevents you from existing as Love.

As you begin removing the barriers inside you to Love, you will start to experience divine Love flowing through you. It will begin to infuse your thoughts, words, and deeds, and you will be on your way to becoming Love.

- **Forgiveness** – Forgiveness is a powerful healing tool. When you forgive someone, it frees you not them. It liberates you from negative emotions such as anger, jealousy, pride, and lust. Do not concern yourself with how the other person chooses to respond to your forgiveness as that is their journey and has nothing to do with you.

  We recommend that you begin by forgiving yourself for the times when you have fallen from grace and have treated yourself or others in a non-Loving way. Forgive yourself, apologize to those that you have slighted, and move on. We also recommend that you forgive everyone that you feel has hurt you in any way. Doing so will free you from a great deal of emotional poison.

  You don't have to think of everything that you need to forgive right away. Start with whatever comes to mind and that will be enough for you to get a feel for the healing power of forgiveness. Move on to step eight and, as you remove the barriers to Love, everything that you need to forgive will rise to the surface.

- **Compassion** – Cultivating compassion begins by seeing the divine in everyone. Most people are identified with the mind and body, and that causes them to function in the world through their fears, beliefs, traumas, and desires. That is a painful way to exist and results in people constantly riding an emotional roller coaster. In essence, they are lost souls who are prisoners of their own conditioned minds. They 'know not what they do'.

  You can choose to see the divine in people rather than react to whatever they are saying or doing. You can feel compassion for them. We recommend that you start with yourself. You have been a prisoner of your own conditioned mind for many years and possibly many lifetimes. You are not going to break free overnight and you are going to fall from grace (respond to external events from your conditioned mind) often on this journey. Be gentle with yourself and have compassion for the beautiful being that you are.

- **Acceptance** - Cultivate acceptance of what is. It is particularly important to accept yourself exactly the way you currently are. That does not mean that you will stay that way forever. It simply means that you are that way now. It is necessary to accept yourself as you currently are because doing so will show you the barriers inside you to Love that need to be removed. We also invite you to accept that everyone else is exactly where they need to be.

- **Gratitude** - Gratitude is life changing. It supports you when you are feeling stuck and enables you to take each step on the journey. Start by cultivating gratitude towards yourself for having the courage to go on this journey. Then, cultivate gratitude towards everyone and everything that comes into your life for giving you the opportunity to find your way 'home'.

7.   Commit to Achieving Inner Peace, Harmony, and Love

This step asks you to make a wholehearted commitment to achieving an inner state of peace, harmony, and Love.

Why are we asking you to make this commitment?

In order to achieve that inner state, you are going to need to remove everything from inside you that is blocking you from having it; all of your inner barriers to divine Love. That may sound simple but it is not always an easy thing to do. In the next step, we are going to show you how to remove those barriers. The process for doing so will ask you to look deep inside yourself and face your inner demons. You are going to need to be totally committed to your inner journey in order to have the determination to face the worst of those demons. You may be able to face many of them without it but you may not be able to face the darkest ones.

Are you ready to commit yourself fully to achieving an inner state of peace, harmony, and Love?

If so, then we recommend that you perform a simple ceremony to reinforce that commitment. Write down your intention to 'achieve an inner state of peace, harmony, and Love' and then read it out loud three times. You may want to do this either in a quiet space in nature or in a room lit with a candle. The setting is not as important as your stating your intention with determination and conviction.

If you are not ready to make this commitment then we suggest that you move on to the next step. You will still be able to remove some of your barriers to Love and each one that you remove will have a Loving effect on you and your life. You will also find that your ability to remain in a state of inner peace will grow to include more and more life situations. Basically, you will become a more peaceful and Loving person. When you come up against your core issues, and become stuck, you can then decide if you are ready to make this commitment.

8.   Look in the Mirror and Remove the Barriers to Love.

This step is your healing journey. It is an ongoing process that you do while living your daily life. It invites you to delve deep inside yourself in order to remove everything that is preventing you from experiencing divine Love flowing through your being.

You do this by treating life as a mirror and using Mindful Awareness to look in that mirror and find your barriers to Love. Finding and removing those barriers is to walk your own unique path 'home' to Love.

The process for finding and removing your barriers to Love is summarized below. For a more detailed description of the process, please refer to volume 2 of The Way Home series of books, 'Self-Healing – Ancient Wisdom Applied to Today's World'. That book describes this process in great detail and also provides step by step instructions for freeing yourself of any pains, illness, and feelings such as those of depression, guilt, loneliness, low self-esteem, and more.

A Choice Point – The monastic life versus the worldly life

Before we go into the process of finding and removing your barriers to Love, we would like to mention that those who are determined to sequester themselves away in order to realize the Self as one with Pure Source Awareness may not need to do this step. The process for becoming one with pure Source Awareness can happen at any time and does not require you to remove your barriers to Love. However, if you do not remove them then any life situation that triggers one of them will disconnect you from Source and thrust you back into your turbulent thoughts and emotions.

You will be what one enlightened master referred to as an 'enlightened asshole'. As long as you are sequestered away somewhere then you can remain in a state of enlightened bliss. However, if you were to come back out into the world then you would be like a ticking time bomb just waiting to go off. Someone would eventually trigger one of your unresolved barriers to Love and you would treat them in a non-Loving way.

Thus, those who are committed to achieving Oneness have a choice to make. Do you wish to remove your barriers to Love and remain in the world at large or do you wish to avoid triggering them by sequestering yourself away?

If you choose to sequester yourself away in a monastery, nunnery, or similar setting then our journey together has likely come to an end. We may, at some point in the future, offer living space for those who wish to be sequestered but, for now, we are focusing on those who wish to remain in the world at large. However, we do honor you for your choice and wish you a life filled with an abundance of ease, grace, and Love. The energy that you radiate out into the world will be of benefit to all and we thank you for being.

If you are choosing to remain in the world at large then our journey continues.

What does it mean to look in the mirror?

Life is the mirror and you are using mindful awareness to observe your inner reaction to external events. When you observe either pain, fear, an emotional reaction such as anger, or a non-Loving thought arising then you know that a barrier inside you to Love has been triggered. You then have the opportunity to delve inside yourself to find and remove that barrier to Love.

Essentially, to look in the mirror is to look at yourself not at the world around you. It is your inner reactions to life's event that matter because they will show you your barriers to Love. You are seeing yourself the way you currently are and we invite you to be completely honest with yourself about what you find. You may not like everything that you discover about yourself. We invite you to accept it anyway. It is only by accepting yourself the way you currently are that you can then find, and remove, the obscurations in your mirror. As the mirror becomes clearer, the essence of who you truly are will come into focus.

Rumi describes the journey into Love as follows:

"Your task is not to seek for love, but merely to seek and find all the barriers within yourself that you have built against it."

You are a being of divine Love and Rumi is asking you to remove the barriers inside you that are preventing you from being what you have always been. He is pointing at the path of Love and is showing you the way 'home'.

So, what are the barriers to Love and how do you find them? A barrier is anything that causes you to disconnect from your true self and throws you into fear, pain, or identification with your thoughts and emotions. The barriers include your fears, conditioned beliefs, emotional traumas, and desires. These barriers lay hidden deep inside you just waiting to be triggered by events in your daily life. Once triggered, the emotions stored with the barrier are brought to the surface and thoughts based on those emotions soon follow. You become lost in your turbulent mind and are disconnected from divine Love.

In order to look in the mirror, you must own your emotions. This cannot be stated strongly enough. It is crucial for you to accept that your emotional reactions are sourced from inside you, not outside, and are pointing at your unresolved barriers to Love. If you blame others for the way you feel then you will become lost in the blame game. You will hold others responsible for your emotions and you will not delve inside to find the true source of your emotions. You will remain a prisoner of your conditioned and fearful mind. At a minimum, please open up to the possibility that all of your emotions are sourced from inside you. You can then proceed with removing your barriers to Love and find out for yourself if it is true for you.

It is time to look in the mirror. Mindful awareness is the tool that enables you to break free from automatically reacting to life from your emotions. It is like a medicine for your mind and soul. It allows you to stay present and to simply observe your inner reactions without responding from them. You are able to stay separate from your fears, pains, emotions, and thoughts. All emotional reactions, including the so-called positive ones such as excitement or happiness, are coming from your barriers to Love. You cannot become lost in your emotions or your thoughts and be Love. You cannot be afraid and be Love.

You become your emotions when you identify with them (e.g. 'I am happy' or 'I am angry'). The alternative to becoming an emotion or thought is to simply observe them while remaining aware of both your inner state of being and external events. You can then enjoy the presence of an emotion such as happiness without getting lost in it. You can also choose whether to act on a thought or to simply let it drift away.

Once you can observe your emotions and your thoughts without becoming lost in them, you are no longer an actor on the stage of life. You are breaking free of engaging with the external world through your fears, conditioning, emotional traumas, and desires. You have learned to be mindfully aware and to use life as a mirror for finding your barriers to Love.

This is a huge breakthrough. You are taking the first steps in discovering who you really are. With this breakthrough, and with the qualities of determination, endurance, honesty, integrity, and patience, you will achieve oneness with Source. You are on your way 'home'.

Please remember that you are not alone during this process. You do have to take responsibility for finding and removing your barriers to Love but others can be there to provide you with Loving support and guidance along the way.

Finding the Barriers to Love

Your internal reactions to life's events are signposts showing you your barriers to Love. Once you have observed such a reaction, the first thing to do is to follow the signpost back down inside yourself to find the barrier itself.

Replay the event that triggered the inner reaction through your mind and let the associated signpost (fear, pain, emotion, or non-Loving thought) grow stronger. Ask your inner guide to show you the source, inside you, of the signpost and then shine the light of awareness on whatever arises. Allow yourself to see the barrier to Love that has been hiding inside you and be willing to accept the truth about yourself no matter what surfaces.

To bring awareness to what is going on inside you in this way is to Love yourself. We call this form of self-Love the 'flame of transformation'. It will burn away all of the illusions that you hold about yourself and it will liberate you from your fears, conditioned beliefs, emotional traumas, and desires. However, it can be extremely challenging to strip yourself naked in this way and you may often feel like you are stepping into a fire.

Rumi cautions that you have to be willing to undress completely in the garden of Love.

> *"If you can't smell the fragrance don't come into the garden of Love. If you're unwilling to undress don't enter the stream of Truth. Stay where you are, don't come our way."*

We have found that the only way to remove one's barriers is to be willing to face everything that surfaces from inside you with openness, honesty, and integrity. You have to be willing to undress completely. However, once something has been brought fully into the light of awareness it can be healed. That is what the garden of Love is all about. We invite you to enter the garden as the reward is immeasurable; direct experiential knowledge of divine Love.

Through cultivating Mindful awareness, looking in the mirror, shining the light of awareness on yourself, and being willing to strip naked, you will be able find the barriers inside you to Love. Doing all of this may sound daunting at first. However, with practice you will find yourself becoming proficient at observing when you have become emotionally charged and then quickly finding the barrier to Love that has been triggered.

Removing the Barriers to Love

Once you are able to find your barriers, the next step is to remove them.

Removing them has the effect of allowing you to experience divine Love. It also has the added bonus of doing preventative maintenance on your body because you will be removing energetic disturbances that could have led to disease. Thus, we refer to the process of removing your barriers as both a journey into Love and a healing journey.

Awareness itself is a powerful healing tool. You will find that you can let many barriers go by simply becoming aware of them. However, there will likely be some fears, beliefs, emotional traumas, and desires that are deeply ingrained in you and require more than awareness to be healed.

For these barriers, you can choose to either heal them yourself or enlist the support of a therapy technique and therapist. We recommend that you allow your inner guide to direct you in either healing yourself alone or healing yourself with the support of a therapy technique.

We have often found that our inner guides would prepare us in advance of a barrier surfacing. We would have been shown the tools and techniques that we were going to need in order to be able to both face the barrier and then heal it. Please remember that the appropriate technique for healing one barrier will likely be different from the approach for the previous one. Do not get caught in the therapy trap; returning for more therapy in the hopes of getting more healing even though the barrier that drew you to that technique has been healed.

Regardless of whether you heal a barrier on your own or with support, you have to do the actual healing. The process for healing each type of barrier to Love is described below.

There is a lie underlying every fear and every belief. You can use insight meditation and trust to find the lie. The fear or false belief will be removed once you stop believing that lie.

For an emotional trauma, you have to feel it to heal it. Use meditation to allow yourself to observe the event that caused the trauma and to feel the associated emotions. While feeling the emotions, use self-Love to accept what happened, forgive everyone involved, learn the soul lessons from the event, and, if necessary, forgive yourself. In order for healing to occur, this forgiveness has to be done while feeling the emotions that you felt at the time of the traumatic event. Mental forgiveness accomplishes no healing.

The last type of barrier, desire, comes from an ego-based need. Use insight meditation and trust to find that need. Once you become aware of the need, you may be able to either let it go or to provide it for yourself. If that doesn't work then use insight meditation and trust to find the fear, belief, or emotional trauma underlying that need. Once you heal that underlying barrier to Love, you can then let go of the need and the original desire will be gone.

At times, it is going to be challenging for you to look at yourself in the mirror and remove your barriers. Please ask for support. You have to do the work but you do not have to do it alone. Those who have gone before you, and those who are travelling alongside you, can support you in allowing an issue to surface, offering guidance in finding the appropriate way to deal with a particular barrier, and providing a Loving environment in which to heal yourself.

A few final words

Removing your barriers to Love is an important part of your journey and we would like to leave you with a few closing words.

A common question that we hear is 'How will I know when I have healed a particular barrier?' This can be a challenge because you will likely find that there are times when you either find more than one barrier associated with a given signpost or you find more than one emotional layer to be healed for a single emotional trauma. You will have to keep going back to the original signpost and follow it back down inside yourself over and over again until all of the barriers associated with that signpost have been healed.

It can be difficult to know when you are finished. One way to know for sure is to watch how you react when an event occurs in your life that is similar to the one that triggered the original inner reaction. If you no longer have the same reaction then you have healed that barrier. A simple example is getting angry when someone cuts you off in traffic. If you have healed this issue then you will find that you do not get angry the next time someone cuts you off.

Adversity will be a part of your journey. Your inner guide is going to be working with you to remove your barriers and that means that it will be creating life situations that allow you to see them. Those life situations will often be emotionally challenging for you. We suggest that you feel grateful for everything that comes into your life. Every event that challenges you is an opportunity to find another barrier to Love. After a while you will find yourself feeling grateful to anyone who can upset you for the gift they are giving you.

You can also use the adversity that you faced in the early years of your life to kick start your journey. You will be able to find barriers to Love by delving into the more difficult moments from your past, and allowing yourself to feel the emotions associated with them.

You may find it overwhelming to be constantly delving into your subconscious wounds and you can ask for your journey to slow down. Your higher self will be bringing situations into your life for you to explore and it will do so at whatever pace you choose. You can ask for things to slow down or speed up. You can even ask for a break. This is your journey and you are in charge of the pace.

As you remove more and more of your barriers to Love, you will be able to abide in an inner state of peace, harmony, and Love more often. Everything that you then say, think, and do will be infused with divine Love and you will be a gift to everyone that you meet. From our experience, you will soon find that you are drawing more Loving people into your life and that your external world begins to reflect your inner state.

This may be the end for you. Parts two and three of the 'Thirteen Steps' are for those who want to go further on the journey of discovering the essence of who they truly are. The steps in those two parts will show you how to surrender to your higher self, fulfill your soul purpose, and have the oceanic experience of becoming one with Source. They will also ask you to let go of your identification with the body, mind, and eventually the soul.

It is your choice to either stop here or move on to part two. Do you want to go on?

?????????

Man cannot connect to God, man must become God.

Part Two: Fulfill your Soul Purpose

9.   Commit to turning control of your Life over to your Higher Self.

In order to go further on the journey of discovering who you are, you are going to have to let go of identifying with the body and mind, and turn control of your life over to your higher self. It is only your higher self that can find, and then fulfill, your soul purpose. In this step, we are asking you to make a commitment to yourself to surrender control of your life to your higher self. This level of commitment will give you the determination required to overcome the obstacles that your mind is going throw at you as it fights to retain control.

Please be aware that making this commitment will put you on a path that will have a profound effect on you and your life. We recommend that you read each of the remaining steps thoroughly before making this commitment.

If you are choosing to commit then we recommend that you perform a simple ceremony. Write down your intention to 'turn control of your life over to your higher self' and then read it aloud three times. You may want to do this in a quiet space in nature, in a room lit only with a candle, or in front of your loved ones. The setting is not as important as your stating your intention with determination and conviction.

This type of commitment is often made after a person experiences a life changing event such as a serious illness, the death of a loved one, a life shattering event, or a beautiful moment in nature when everything falls silent inside. These kinds of events are often referred to as a 'call' from the soul to return 'home'. Once a person chooses to answer a 'call' then there is no turning back. We are often asked if a life shattering event is necessary prerequisite for someone to have the determination required to embark upon this journey and the answer is no. Making this commitment has the same effect.

10. Accept that spiritual madness is a normal part of the journey 'home' and that the madness can be passed through.

Most people who attempt to go beyond the mind will go through one or more phases of spiritual madness.

Your commitment to turn control of your life over to your higher self will have been an invitation to your inner guide to make that happen. You will have set in motion the events that will guide you in liberating yourself from identification with the mind and then fulfilling your soul purpose. Your job will be to tune into your inner guide at all times and to follow its guidance no matter what.

As you begin to follow your inner guide, a conflict will likely ensue between the logical reasoning of your rational mind and the guidance that you are receiving from your inner guide. This is a battle for control of your life between your rational mind and your higher self. If you are determined to turn control of your life over to your higher self then it is eventually going to win this war. However, your rational mind is likely to win many of the skirmishes along the way. This inner war can, and often does, lead to spiritual madness.

This internal conflict intensifies as you stop playing the roles that others have thrust upon you and instead connect back to your higher self. The chattering of your fearful and conditioned mind gets louder and you struggle to hear what your inner guide is saying over the noise inside your own head. You want to connect back to your higher self but you can't hear it, and a madness sets in at the separation you feel from who you really are. This is a 'normal' part of the journey of reconnecting to the divine within and is often referred to as the 'Dark Night of the Soul'.

This is a time on your journey when you need to feel absolutely determined to find your way 'home' no matter the cost. This is why we invited you to make the commitment in the previous step. When your spiritual madness arises, embrace it and allow yourself to fall all the way through it. If you pull yourself out of the madness, through taking on a new role or a new belief system, then you will be right back where you started. Remember, it is always darkest before the dawn.

The most important thing that you can do when you are faced with spiritual madness is to continue to cultivate your connection with your inner guide. Be open to it 'speaking' to you in ways that you could not have previously conceived. It may be trying to reach you through simple means such as a sign on a bus or through the person you meet in a coffee shop. If you cling to any ideas of how you are 'supposed' to be communicating with your inner guide then you are likely missing a great deal of the guidance that you are being given.

The dark night can be challenging and we suggest that you lean on your fellow travelers for support. They are not there to take away your madness but rather to provide you with a loving environment while you pass through it. Living your life with the energies of acceptance, gratitude, and trust will ease the journey.

Also, we recommend that you let go of any spiritual ambitions that you may have. Fantasies about how spiritual you are going to become are created by your rational mind and holding on to them will keep you stuck in the madness. Lastly, let go of any fears that you may have of what your soul may ask you to do with your life once you connect back to it. It may be something seemingly menial to you or it may be something that feels grandiose. Either way, trust that you will be ready to do whatever is asked of you.

One day you will wake up and find that the madness has simply ended. You will have done nothing to 'get rid of the madness'. You will have simply strengthened your connection with your inner guide and your mind will have let go of its frustration at not knowing what is coming next in your life. You will be in the flow of life. You will have passed through the 'Dark night of the Soul'.

11. Surrender Control of your life to your Higher Self.

This is the step in which you let go of all identification with the body and mind, and surrender control of your life to your higher self. You will then be living your life by acting on divine inspiration, or 'Divine Will', and responding to everything that comes into your life from a space of divine Love.

The process of letting go of identification with the body and mind includes dropping your attachment to the concept of 'free will'. In order to surrender to your eternal self, you need to drop the 'you' that thinks it has free will. 'You' do have free will but only when 'you' are under the illusion that you are the body and mind. 'Free will' is a creation of the mind to serve the mind and only has meaning when you are functioning in the world with the servant, your rational mind, in charge. When you surrender control of your life to your higher self, you are effectively surrendering to 'Divine will'.

This is a very simple step to execute and likely one of the most challenging things that you will do. It typically feels like a scary fall into a black and empty nothingness because that is the way the mind often perceives the realm beyond the mind. It may even feel like a death to you and, in a way, it is. It is the death of identifying yourself with the rational mind. You will need to have cultivated a high level of trust in your inner guide in order to take this step. It is only the combination of trust and fierce determination that will give you the willingness to face the fear of death and fall into the unknown.

We suggest that you start by giving control over small parts of your life to your higher self so that you can feel what it is like to have your higher self in charge of your life. For example, you could go on a trip with no preset plans and trust that 'divine will' will guide you to the appropriate places along the way. In this way, you can test your ability to thrive in the gap between the limited and controlled 'known' world of the rational mind, and the expansive 'unknown' world that awaits you. As you become more and more comfortable living in this gap, you are preparing yourself to surrender your entire life to the divine within.

Obstacles to Overcome

There are a few hurdles that you may have to overcome before you will be able to take this step.

One of the many joys of this journey is that it will open you up to the mysteries of life. You may find yourself 'remembering' latent abilities such as clairvoyance, clairsentience, recalling past lives, 'seeing' energy instead of form, astral travel, and much more. These experiences can be rather mind blowing, in a beautiful way, and they will have lessons to teach you about who you really are. However, it is important to remember not to get caught in the trap of trying to repeat them. If you do that then these experiences can become distractions that may slow down, or even derail, your journey. We suggest that you embrace these magical experiences when they come into your life, take the lessons that they are offering, and move on.

Be careful of developing a spiritual ego. Humility is a key trait to foster throughout this journey. Without humility, you can get caught up in thinking that you are a spiritual seeker, that you have 'special' spiritual abilities, that you are some kind of spiritual 'master', or that you are a renunciate. Everything that you think you are is akin to a prison cell that will keep you stuck in the world of the ego; in this case, the spiritual ego. To complete this step, you will need to drop all of the roles that you have been playing, let go of any specialness that you feel about yourself, and let go of identifying with anything that is experienced through the mind. Cultivating humility allows you to do that and hastens your journey 'home'. Those who embrace being last in the world of ego will be first in discovering their divine selves.

One of the final hurdles that you may face in being able to surrender to your higher self is the belief that you would do nothing without the rational mind telling you what to do. You may 'think' that you will simply sit on your couch, or retreat into a cave, for the rest of your life. That couldn't be further from the truth. Once you have surrendered to your higher self, you will simply be acting from divine inspiration rather than from rational thinking.

We recommend that you adopt the following three step process for overcoming this hurdle. It will give you the opportunity to experience having divine inspiration guide your life.

1. ***Act from divine inspiration.*** Allow divine Love to function through you by acting on whatever you feel divinely inspired to do. You will only be able to do this from a purely divine space after you have dropped identification with the mind and body. Until then, any inspiration you receive may be either coming from your mind or being filtered through your mind. Either way, it will not be infused solely with divine Love. However, you can still practice acting from a space of divine inspiration until you are ready to drop your identification with the mind. At that point, acting from inspiration will become your natural state of being.

2. ***Do not be attached to the fruits of your actions.*** Do not try to figure out with your mind why you are doing anything and do not be attached to any specific outcome. Simply act upon your divine inspiration and allow divine Love to infuse everything that you think, say, and do.

3. ***Flow with Life.*** Respond to external events from an inner space of divine Love. You can cultivate this ability by bringing mindful awareness to every moment of your life in order to ensure that you respond from Love rather than from the machinations of the mind. Once you have gone beyond the mind, you will automatically respond from a space of divine Love, and will no longer need mindful awareness.

Once you have turned control of your life over to your higher self, this three-step process will be your natural way of functioning in the world. It will be like breathing to you. At that point, you will have become the phrase, 'Life is Divine Love in action'.

The last challenge that we wish to share with you is the fear of accepting that you are a divine being of immense power. Marianne Williamson describes this fear as follows:

"Our deepest fear is not that we are inadequate. Our deepest fear is that we are powerful beyond measure. It is our light, not our darkness that most frightens us." (2)

Face that fear by accepting that you may very well be a divine being of immense power. Drop your identification with the mind and surrender to the divine being that you are. By doing so, you will go beyond this world and will be free; free of your own fearful and conditioned mind. You will be a beacon of light amidst a sea of darkness. Everything that you say, think, and do, will be infused with divine Love and your very presence will stir the divine to awaken in others. Your life will be a blessing to all beings.

12. Fulfill your 'Soul Purpose'

If you have a soul purpose then you will need to fulfill it. It is theoretically possible that a soul could incarnate without a specific purpose, and be here solely to remove all of its barriers to Love. However, we have found that most people do have a soul purpose.

A soul purpose is very different from the quest that many are on to find the 'meaning of life'. That quest is typically for the meaning of 'my' life and, as long as 'I' am identified with the mind and body, then that search will be fruitless. The mind is simply a tool for the soul to use in order to function in the realm of form and it does not have a meaning unto itself. Similarly, the ego does not have a meaning as it is created in the mind and is simply a set of fears, conditioned beliefs, emotional traumas, and desires. Thus, as long as you are identified with the mind and body then you have no purpose; other than to learn your soul lessons and drop that identification. However, once you move beyond the body and mind, a whole new world opens up to you and that world may well include a soul purpose.

So, what is a soul purpose? When a soul chooses to incarnate, it typically does so with the intention of completing a specific task. That task is what we refer to as your soul purpose.

Once you reach this step on your inner journey, you will likely find that you are feeling drawn to act in the world in response to divine inspiration. However, you may also feel like something else is bubbling around inside you wanting to come out. That something else is your soul purpose. You will feel restless until you complete it. In a way, having a soul purpose is akin to being in bondage because you are not free to act solely from divine Love until you have fulfilled it.

Finding your Soul Purpose

Your soul purpose is likely to be related to either being of service to others or creating something beautiful. The process of fulfilling it will invariably infuse you with joy. Your inner guide is the only one who knows your soul purpose. Fortunately, to get this far on your journey, you will have cultivated a strong trust in your inner guide and it will once again be time to lean on that trust.

There are many different ways to find your soul purpose and they generally involve secluding yourself away in a silent space so that your inner guide can show it to you. One of the common results of doing something like a vision quest, walkabout, or safari is to be given a glimpse of one's soul purpose. We suggest that you try one of these activities, or some other form of deep meditative retreat, with the intention of finding your soul purpose. During the retreat, allow your mind to fall silent and trust that your inner guide will show you what you are ready to see. You may find that you are only given glimpses of the overall purpose at first. Be patient as your inner guide will reveal your purpose to you at a pace that is most appropriate for you.

It is important to note that you do not need to complete all of the previous steps, including the steps in part one, before finding your soul purpose. You may receive hints as to what it is throughout your journey and you may feel drawn to do something like a vision quest at any point. Whenever you feel inspired to discover your soul purpose, trust that you are ready to see it and allow yourself to be guided to it.

Fulfilling your Soul Purpose

Your soul purpose can only be completed by your higher self. It is important to remember that it doesn't belong to your rational mind and that any attempt to complete it by your rational mind will be doomed to failure. You will only be able to accomplish your soul purpose when you can allow your divine self to function through you without your rational mind getting in the way. As long as you 'think' that your soul purpose is something that 'you' (as the mind and body) have to do then you cannot do it.

You fulfill your soul purpose by:

- accepting it no matter how daunting it may feel to your rational mind;

- setting the intention to complete it;

- trusting that your higher self will bring everything into your life that you need in order to complete it;

- acting on divine inspiration;

- not being attached to the outcome of your actions (including the completion of your soul purpose);

- allowing divine Love to infuse everything that you think say, and do;

- flowing with life by responding to external events from an inner space of divine Love; and,

- being patient.

The process of fulfilling your soul purpose may trigger unresolved barriers to Love related to 'helping' others. Your 'job' will then be to remove those barriers while patiently waiting for your soul purpose to be fulfilled through simply allowing divine Love to live you. You will likely find that there are fewer and fewer barriers to be removed and that, for the most part, you are able to exist in the world with a feeling of deep inner peace.

Once your soul purpose has been completed then you are no longer bound to this world. You are free to act from divine inspiration and to respond to life's events from an inner space of divine Love.

"Returning to the Source is stillness. Which is the way of nature. The way of nature is unchanging."

— Lao Tzu

Part Three: Achieve Self-Realization

13. Realize the Self as One with Pure Source Awareness.

There is one more surrender to go; the ultimate surrender.

Your higher self, or soul, was seeded from pure Source awareness and is separate from it. In order to have the oceanic experience of becoming One with all that is, you will have to let go of identifying with your higher self and merge back into pure Source awareness.

Kabir is referring to the knowledge that is attained through returning to Source in the following quote:

"Many know that the drop merges into the ocean, few know that the ocean merges into the drop."

When you merge back into pure Source awareness, it merges with you. You become one with everything, and you are the field of awareness that is infusing everything in this world of form. You are everywhere at once and 'you' are no longer there. Awareness simply is.

We can guide you in creating the appropriate conditions in which the opportunity to merge with Source will arise, but only you can do it. Only you can die before you die. The inner state of being that invites in the experience of Oneness is a silent mind, a heart free of all desire, and a state of complete physical relaxation. Patiently abiding in that inner state of being, and following any guidance from your inner guide, is all that one can do.

We have not found words to adequately describe what you will go through as you make this final surrender. All we can suggest is that you open to the divine and allow it to pour in. However, those words do not do it justice and you are best served by simply trusting that your inner guide will show you the way.

You can have this oceanic experience before leaving the body. At first, you may find yourself connecting to pure Source Awareness for very brief moments and then being returned to the world of form. It can be a disconcerting feeling to be back in this world and you may wonder what to do. There will be nothing to do. You may have returned in order to be of service to others or you may have had a brief connection to pure Source awareness prior to having completed your soul purpose. Either way, allow yourself to remain in the world but not be of the world. Act from divine inspiration and flow with life.

Congratulations! You have experienced 'Oneness'. You have found your way 'home'. Many would say that this is the greatest accomplishment that a person can achieve. You may have waited many, many lifetimes for this moment. You may still be waiting to complete your soul purpose but you will know, from your own direct experience, who you are. You will be free of all illusions and all suffering. You will be 'home'.

"Relax, life is a journey to be enjoyed not a struggle to be endured.".

In Closing

There are no more steps. That's it. We close with a common question and a few final words.

Do I need a Spiritual Master?

We are often asked if it is appropriate to follow a spiritual master. Our answer is always the same, that is totally up to you. A spiritual master is not needed but a master may greatly expedite your journey.

For the purposes of this book, a spiritual master is one who is either said to be enlightened or to have knowledge of the truth. We feel that the choice to spend time with a 'master' is one to be taken with great care. You give your power over to a master when you choose to follow them and, therefore, we feel that it is not a decision to be taken lightly. Trust your intuition. If it feels appropriate for you to become a disciple of a master then that is your choice. We simply invite you to be wary of false masters. In the words of Rumi.

> *"The one who cuts of your head is your friend.*
> *The one who puts it back is a deceiver.*
> *The one who weighs you with his troubles is your burden.*
> *But the one who loves you will set you free".*

Seek out spiritual masters who would 'cut off your head' by disconnecting you from your rational mind and pointing you towards your inner guide. Avoid those who would either feed your rational mind with some kind of belief system (put your head back on), give you some kind of pleasant sensory experience (put your head back on), or ask you for something (trouble you).

When you bring your awareness to something then you are focusing the energy of Love on it. Look for a 'master' who will Love you ('the one who loves you will set you free') by assisting you in becoming aware of what is happening inside you and points you back towards who you really are.

Find out for yourself if all of this is true for you

We ask you not to 'believe' anything that you read in this book. This program is not a belief system. It is a set of tools and techniques for those who want to 'know' through their own direct experience. It is not for those who wish to follow a person or scripture that would tell them what to believe.

Welcome

Welcome to 'The Way Home'. This is a living program that will evolve as we evolve. It belongs to everyone.

Glossary

Words often have different meanings to different people. These are the
definitions of some of the key words and phrases that are used in this book.
The definitions of these words may not match either the dictionary
definition or your definition.

Barriers to Love – The barriers to Love are the four components of the
ego; fears, desires, beliefs, and emotional traumas. They are called barriers
to Love because a human being cannot be functioning from one of these
barriers and be Love.

Divine Love (a.k.a. Love) – Divine Love is the energy of pure Source
awareness and of the soul. Love will only flow through a human being
when they have fallen silent inside and have gone beyond their ego-mind.
This form of Love is healing.

Ego (a.k.a. ego-mind) – The ego is a person's set of fears, beliefs, desires,
and emotional traumas. Functioning from any one of these four
components of the ego results in a person becoming disconnected from
Love.

Ego-Mind (a.k.a. ego) – See Ego.

False Self – The false self includes the ego-mind and the physical body. It
is so-called because identifying oneself with the false self prevents a
human being from knowing who they really are.

Heart-based love – Heart-based love is other centered. It is about
imposing your ego's beliefs of what is best for another person onto them.
It is a game of the ego and there is no healing power in this form of love.

Higher Self (a.k.a. Inner Guide and Soul) – The Higher Self is the eternal
aspect of your being that resides beyond the ego-mind and body. It is
seeded from pure Source Awareness and carries the energy of divine Love.
It is also called your soul or inner guide.

Home – Home is an inner state of being that is silent, peaceful, and joyful.
It is attained through cultivating a relaxed body, a silent mind, and a quiet
heart. It is the state of being that enables the energy of divine Love to flow
through a person and out into the world.

Inner Guide (a.k.a. Higher Self and Soul) – Your Inner Guide is the eternal aspect of your being that resides beyond the ego-mind and body. It is seeded from pure Source Awareness and carries the energy of divine Love. It is also called your soul or higher self.

Insight Meditation – Insight Meditation is a technique for having your inner guide provide you with insights on a specific question or intention. It is performed by focusing on the question you would like to ask and then using any meditation practice to enter into a meditative state. You then simply wait for your inner guide to provide the answer.

Looking in the Mirror – Looking in the Mirror is to use mindful awareness to observe your inner reaction to life's events. You observe when any fear, anger (and any other emotion), or pain arises inside you. You also observe when you are triggered into reacting from a non-Loving motivation such as wanting to be right or espousing a belief. Fear, anger, pain, and a non-Loving motivation are the signposts indicating that a barrier to Love inside you has been triggered and that you have some self-healing to do.

Love (a.k.a. Divine Love) - – (Upper case) Love is the energy of pure Source awareness and of the soul. Love can flow through a human being when they have fallen silent inside and have gone beyond their ego-mind. This form of Love is healing.

love – (Lower case) love is ego-based. The two types of love that have been created by the ego are mind-based love and heart-based love. These forms of love are games of the ego and have no Love in them. There is no healing power in love.

Meditation – Meditation is a state of being. Meditation is the art of shifting your awareness to ever subtler levels of awareness while remaining aware of the previous levels.

Mind-based love – Mind-Based love is what we are referring to when we say things such as 'I love chocolate because it tastes good' or 'I love you because you make me happy'. Mind-based love is all about what your ego gains from getting what it wants. It is a game of the ego and there is no healing power in this form of love.

Mindful Awareness – Mindful Awareness is to be aware of everything going on, both inside you and outside of you, in the present moment without reacting to it. You simply observe it.

Pure Source Awareness (a.k.a. Source) – Pure Source Awareness is a field of awareness that permeates everything in this world of form. It is the One that we all return to when we let go of identification with both the false self and the higher self. It has been referred to by many belief systems with terms such as the Holy Spirit, Source, Tao, Universal Consciousness, God, and the Supreme Self.

Self-Love – Self-Love is to accept yourself exactly as you are without judgment. You accept the way you feel, the motivation for your thoughts, words, and actions, your inner emotions and demons, your ailments, and your body. Accepting yourself does not mean that you have to stay the same way forever. It just means that you are accepting yourself as you are today. Self-Love opens the door to healing. Unless you can accept something, you cannot heal it.

Soul (a.k.a. Higher Self and Inner Guide) - The soul is the eternal aspect of your being that resides beyond the ego-mind and body. It is seeded from pure Source Awareness and carries the energy of divine Love. It is also called your higher self or inner guide.

Source (a.k.a. pure Source awareness) – a field of awareness that permeates everything in this world of form. It is the One that we all return to when we let go of identification with both the false self and the higher self. It has been referred to by many belief systems with terms such as the Holy Spirit, Tao, Universal Consciousness, God, and the Supreme Self.

Trust – Trust is to trust in your inner guide only. Do not trust your ego-mind, anyone else's ego-mind, nor any form of external God. Your inner guide will bring the situations into your life that you need in order to learn your soul lessons, and it will guide you towards the life you incarnated to live. It will also enable you to find and remove your barriers to Love.

Bibliography

1. Samples, Bob, "Bob Samples Quotes", goodreads.com. Web. Accessed on February 27, 2015, <http://www.goodreads.com/author/quotes/84371.Bob_Samples>

2. Williamson, Marianne, <u>A Return to Love: Reflections on the Principles of A Course in Miracles</u>, Page #190. HarperCollins Publishers LLC, New York, New York, 1St Edition (1992). © 1992.

Other Books by Bruce Taylor

Self-Healing: Ancient Wisdom Applied to Today's World.

Communities of the Future: The Universal Download.

Available in print and kindle format at: amazon.com/author/taylorbruce

About the Author

Bruce currently lives on Cortes Island in British Columbia with his wife, son, and a few friends. He provides service to others through acting as a spiritual guide. A spiritual guide is one who has connected to his or her own inner guide and can support others in connecting to their own inner guide. He offers one on one guidance, facilitated discussions, and awareness retreats.

Bruce lived in a Tibetan Bon monastery in India where he studied under a Dzogchen master and has combined what he learned there with Peruvian Shamanism and Zen principles to create a program for awakening people from the western mind. The program is called 'The Way Home'. It provides people with guidance in removing the barriers inside themselves to being Love, support in discovering and fulfilling their reason for incarnating, and guidance in creating the inner state of being that invites in the oceanic experience of Oneness.

He has also been gifted with a vision of how communities of the future are going to be formed. This vision is one that has been received by many people around the world. He feels inspired to be a part of creating those communities and thereby heralding a Golden Age for humanity. However, he also knows that any effort on his part to actually create a community will fail. He is simply trusting that one will manifest if it is meant to.

Bruce can be contacted at **brucejtaylor@yahoo.com**.

23337036R00026

Made in the USA
Columbia, SC
11 August 2018